WALK
SOUT
AND IONA

by
Olive Brown
and
Jean Whittaker

GRIBUN

Brown & Whittaker
1996 Revised and expanded

1

Carsaig Cliffs from Scoor

CONTENTS

Public Road	═
Route of Walk	.....
Bridge	⊔
Gate	⊢⊣
Summit	△
Deciduous Trees	♈
Coniferous Trees	♣
Viewpoint	ⱨ
Fence	+++++
Dun	⁂

© Olive M. Brown and E. Jean Whittaker, 1987

A CODE FOR MULL

1. Gates

Farmers say that when walkers cross their land, gates cause more problems than anything else, so we would ask, on their behalf, that you respect these rules:

1. If you find a gate open, leave it open.
2. If you find a gate closed, shut it after you again, securely fastened and stockproof.
3. If you find a gate locked or tied up with string or wire, please don't try to open it. Climb it at the hinge end.

2. Dogs:

Dogs also cause problems for farmers so we would ask you to keep your dog under control where there are animals and to take special note of the lambing season (March-May), when sheep should not be disturbed. If you find any animal in distress such as an apparently lost lamb or a sheep stuck on a ledge, report it, do not attempt to deal with it yourself.

3. Deer:

Most of south Mull is stalked. Difficulties between stalkers and walkers usually arise through simple ignorance and lack of awareness that deer form an important part of the Highland economy, just as sheep do. There are only a few walks in this book where the walker is likely to come into conflict with the stalking interest and these have been indicated. The walker in Scotland enjoys a most enviable freedom. In order that that freedom may continue for the sake of other walkers, we have suggested that certain walks be avoided altogether for a restricted period during the height of the stalking season. Thereafter, some culling takes place and it might be advisable to check with the appropriate landowner whether stalking is in progress. A rifle bullet travels three miles - you could get shot!

4. Go carefully on single-track roads. The passing places are for vehicles to pass or to allow overtaking. Never park there or anywhere where it is likely to cause difficulty of access to farmers' fields.

5. Respect wildlife, plants and trees and guard against fire.

6. Leave no litter.

Ben More and the Chioch from the Glen road.

4

INTRODUCTION

Hills, glens, rocky coasts, sandy beaches - the south part of the island of Mull offers the walker a great variety of routes and scenery. With such richness to choose from it is, perhaps, not easy to know where to start. This book gives a selection of different walks ranging from the lonely hills of central Mull to the gentle island of Iona. Each walk has been thoroughly explored by the authors and a sketch map and an indication of the time taken is given. This timing is fairly generous, allowing for stops to admire the view or even where necessary, to catch your breath! Taking along an Ordnance Survey map of the area will be useful, either the Landranger Series (Sheets 48 and 49) or better still for walking, the Pathfinder Series (Sheets 329, 330, 341, 342, 343 and 353).

Although geology shapes the scenery everywhere, here in south Mull there are dramatic contrasts round every corner. The evidence of a landscape formed by volcanic eruptions and moulded by glaciers is everywhere to be seen, scarcely softened by man. Geological curiosities abound in south Mull, the best known being the Carsaig Arches and MacCulloch's Tree. Whilst the geological structure forms the bones of the island, the pattern of land use has changed and is changing. The vast crofting population of the nineteenth century has gone, their inheritors are the farmers and estate owners of today, with fish farming the latest addition to the economy. Subsistence farming has been replaced by a type of farming which aims at a quality market - prime Scotch beef, lamb, venison and salmon. It is worth remembering that the wide open spaces beloved of the walker are in use. In particular, sporting estates must be managed like any other business. There is little hardship in avoiding the hills during the height of the stalking season when Mull has coastal walking second to none, and we would ask you to read most carefully note 3 on Deer in the Code for Mull on page 4.

Of the many coastal walks in south Mull and Iona, no two are alike and each is rewarding in its own way, whether it has dramatic cliffs or gentle wooded shores. The sea is never very far away, even when on an inland walk, and views to other distant islands can be seen from many vantage points.

Even on the best of summer days, it is advisable to wear sturdy footwear, as much of the land is peaty and boggy and the coastal walking can be very rough. A waterproof jacket and an extra sweater should be carried against a sudden change of weather as some of the walks take you into remote country. If you have a car, please park it thoughtfully, not in a passing place, on the road or in a farmer's gateway.

The descriptions of the walks may mention things of the past by way of interest, such as deserted villages or legends of ancient feuds, but the island of Mull is alive and growing, and a place of work to its inhabitants - please do not jeopardise anyone's livelihood by careless behaviour. We are indebted to the farmers and landowners over whose land you will pass, and we must thank them for their co-operation and helpful advice. Please read the Code for Mull . . . and enjoy your walking!

Olive Brown
Jean Whittaker

Tobermory
April 1987

1. Glen More

Glen More is the gateway for what is indisputably south Mull, the Ross and the Firth of Lorn coast. The present road through the glen dates from the early 1970s and, from entering the glen after Loch Spelve, to emerging from the confines of the glen at the cottage at Craig, it is possible to walk nearly all the of the 7½ miles on the old road. We recommend it to walkers who enjoy a good march (in summer the Iona bus passes every two hours for the weary or those wanting to do it in one direction only). The Iona road enters the glen just past Loch Spelve. A little beyond the turn-off to Lochbuie and Croggan, there is a cattle grid and, just short of this, it is possible to take the car down onto the old road to park. The road follows the valley of the Lussa through well-grown forestry for nearly two miles. About three-quarters of a mile upstream is the Pedlar's Pool, where there is a memorial to the pedlar John Jones, who died of smallpox contracted when selflessly nursing a stricken family on his round. After the old road emerges from the trees, it keeps intermittent company with the new road until the cottage of Craig is reached. This is the place to get the very best view of Ben More.

The heart of the glen may be said to be around the chain of three lochs which are visible from the road. In the nearest of these lochs is an island. This island is a prehistoric construction known as a crannog, being wholly or partly artificial. It is associated with the character of Eoghann a Chinn Bhig (Ewan of the Little Head) who figures at the centre of Mull's creepiest supernatural story. Ewan, son and heir of Lochbuie, lived in a castle on this island with his wife, who was forever nagging him to obtain more land (and, no doubt, a more salubrious dwelling place) from his father. Lochbuie proved unforthcoming. High words passed, Ewan struck him and a clan battle was in the making. On the eve of battle, Ewan met up with a fairy woman and asked her his destiny. The reply, predictably, was enigmatic: if Ewan's wife offered him butter and cheese before the battle - unasked and with her own hand all would be well. If not, Ewan would die. On the morning of battle, both Ewan and his wife ran true to form: his wife stayed in bed and Ewan, foolish to the last, waited in vain for the loving words until he could delay no longer but went out to face his father and his father's ally, MacLean of Duart on the battlefield. There, as foretold, he was killed, his head sliced from his shoulders by a claymore and his headless trunk, still upright in the stirrups, was carried by his terrified horse to the ford of the Lussa, where the body finally fell out of the saddle.

As an alternative to walking the whole route, this sequence of events may be followed by walking from Ishriff to Torness along the old road. Start above the isolated cottage of Ishriff - the island in the loch is clearly visible from here, and as you walk the mile and a quarter to the bend in the road, you retrace Ewan's ride to his destiny; the battle is thought to have taken place somewhere in the flat land around the bend and the hillock of Ceann Chnocain. As you turn the bend towards Torness, you may imagine the decapitated body of the unfortunate Ewan being borne towards the ford of the Lussa. There, buried in the heather on the right of the path that leads down to the ford, you may see the cairn that Ewan's servants built on the spot where he fell to earth. His corpse was conveyed to Iona where it was buried though hardly laid to rest - Ewan still rides abroad in the southern parts of Mull and the sight or sound of the headless horsemen is said to presage a death amongst the family of the MacLaines of Lochbuie.

By way of a more pleasant ending to this tale of horror, the walker might like to go a little downstream from the ford of the Lussa (now bridged) and admire the Falls of the Lussa - a noted spot to see salmon running.

From above Ishriff in the opposite direction the old road goes westwards past Clach Sguabain, a huge boulder thrown from Loch Spelve during the course of an argument between Fingalian giants, according to legend. The rest of the walk on the old road to Craig gives a sense of the loneliness of the glen that is not easily appreciated driving through in a bus or a car. The glen is narrow here, the hills crowd in and there are some fine bands of cliffs high above. Deer are often seen grazing quite near to the road. Eagles and buzzards may well be seen soaring above.

Loch Spelve

2. Croggan

A gentle coastal walk along the shores of a sheltered sea loch, mostly on a quiet road. Loch Spelve, almost landlocked and girt with bracken-clad hills might have been lifted from the Trossachs or the Lake District.

Start at Kinlochspelve at the junction on the Craignure to Lochbuie road signposted to Croggan. You may, of course, shorten this walk by any distance you desire by driving part, or all of the way to Croggan but the road is pleasant, fringed with birch trees and is easy level walking following the coastline all the way past Croggan Pier. Across the waters of Loch Spelve are the buildings of a fish farm, whose cages can be seen on the loch, one of the many now established in quiet sea lochs around the west coast of Scotland. Beyond Croggan, the road becomes a track, bottomed with the rounded pebbles of the raised beach over which it runs. Not far from Croggan there is an amazing perched block, just like a mushroom, a little below HW mark. Out in the channel the water is in a constant state of motion, funnelled in and out of the narrow entrance at a rate of four knots springs. A white spot on a rock on the opposite shore is a navigation mark for boats negotiating the entrance: in days gone by MacBrayne's steamers came into the loch for a scheduled stop at Croggan pier.

Follow the track past a sandy beach to where it ends at a house called Portfield. As you work along the Firth of Lorn, there are views across the Firth towards Kerrera and the hills south of Oban.

These may be better appreciated by climbing up the hill - Maol Buidhe - behind Portfield where the track ends. From the top of this grassy dome, a wide sweep of the Firth of Lorn may be seen from Lismore round to the Garvellochs.

Continue across the high ground towards the mouth of Loch Spelve and descend to the deserted villages of Barnashoag and Balgamrie, which show evidence of having been quite large communities. Continue across the high ground taking a line on Cruach Ardura, the small knobbly hill which rises straight from the waters of Loch Spelve. This course will bring you out above the houses of Croggan and so back along the road to your starting point.

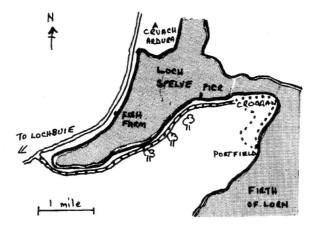

3. Glen Forsa

8 miles, 3 hours

This walk takes you from the outskirts of Salen through to the Glen More road and is almost entirely level. Though barely 8 miles on foot, the journey round by car is at least nineteen miles. It is possible to do this walk as a two-car expedition or by using the buses to return to your car.

Leave the A849 Salen to Craignure road just where it splits briefly into a dual carriageway, a mile beyond Salen near the Glenforsa Hotel. The straight track runs side by side with the Forsa river most of the way. The river is one of the best salmon rivers in Mull, with gravelly holding pools where, in dry weather, the salmon lie deep in the peaty water. After about a mile, the track passes through a gate with a stile for walkers. Ahead is the steep cone of Ben Talaidh where the wreckage of a wartime plane still lies in the central gully (see page 10).

Two miles on, the track runs uphill, goes through a ford and then forks. From this slight rise look back down the glen, a classic example of a U-shaped glaciated valley with its abundant moraines.

The right hand fork leads up to the bothy at Tomsleibhe belonging to the Mountain Bothy Association, and on to the gruelling pass through to Loch Ba, but bear left to continue through Glen Forsa. Another gate leads into a plantation and the forestry track continues for some distance before giving way to a well trodden path and another gate. After a mile you will reach an electric fence where a gate will take you out on to the open hill at a block of open ground left as a corridor for deer commuting between the two hills. Just beyond this the hillside bends away back into the Coire Ghaibhre. Walk along the contour above the fence until you reach a place where two burns from this corrie meet and plunge into a deep gorge crossed by the fence. Make your way a little upstream to cross both burns, then re-enter the plantation by another gate. Lower down the burn can be seen the remains of some ruined cottages where several families once lived. From here follow the burn down as far as the second ruined cottage, turn right, and follow the ride through the forest until you come to another spur of forestry track which will take you the last half mile to the road. This is a convenient place to park if walking from the opposite direction, but starting from the Salen end gives more interesting views of Ben Talaidh and of remote corries on the far side of the glen.

4. Ben Talaidh
763m, 2502 ft

Stalking: Contact DAFS, D MacGillivray 01680 300335

H MacPhail 01680 300424

This lovely, cone-shaped mountain is easily recognised from many viewpoints in Mull and can be climbed from either a north or south approach. From its steep sides flow the burns that feed three rivers systems: the Forsa, the Ba and the Lussa. Its short turf is a delight to walk on in dry conditions: in wet, it leads to many an impromptu glissade!

Ascent from the north

The Tomsleibhe bothy, four miles up Glen Forsa, marks the beginning of the ascent. The bothy is a good place to pause and sign the bothy book after the long walk in before setting off for the summit. The easiest line of ascent is the most obvious - the walker crosses the Allt nan Clar and follows the north ridge to the top, pausing from time to time to look back down the glaciated valley of the Forsa and beyond to the Sound of Mull.

At 2502 feet, Ben Talaidh just makes it as the lower of Mull's two Corbetts, but take note that it is the cairn, 25m SW of the trig pillar that marks the summit. Routes down can be either by retracing the ascent route, or by picking your way down over the scree on the east side to the shoulder and then following the Allt nan Clar down Glen Lean back to the bothy. The bed of this burn is scattered with the remains of a Dakota that crashed during the war. The plane was a Dakota DC3 on a flight from Canada to Prestwick. On 1st February 1945, unable to maintain altitude due to severe air frame icing, it clipped the summit of the mountain and slid down the north side. Of the eight people aboard, three were killed and one died subsequently. A massive

Ben Talaidh from Torness

rescue operation was mounted with the help of navy personnel from the large wartime base at Tobermory. For some time the plane remained on the slope of the hill, relatively intact but, after some years, a decision was made to blow up the wreck and the remains were pushed down to the bed of the Allt nan Clar. A memorial scroll with information about this tragedy is displayed in the entrance hall of Salen School and some fragments are in the Mull Museum in Tobermory.

Ascent from Glen More

The ascent from the south avoids a long walk in. Ben Talaidh is the third highest hill on Mull after Ben More (966m) and Dun da Ghaoithe (766m) but any route to its summit is short and steep. Start at the forestry track half-a-mile west of the ruin of Torness on the long bend in the A849 in Glen More. Walk up the north bank of the Abhainn Doir a Mhaim keeping to the edge of the trees until you reach a stile which gives access to the open hillside. From here it is a very steep pull up onto the ridge. As you walk round the curve of the ridge, the three river valleys lead the eye away to the distant sea. Now a steady ascent of about 700 feet brings you out onto the rounded top with its trig pillar and cairn.

The descent can be varied by following the route past the Dakota then back along Glen Forsa to Glen More as described on page 9.

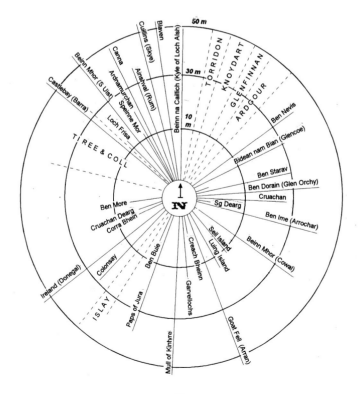

5. Dun da Ghaoithe Ridge

12 miles

An all day excursion

This classic ridge walk is one of the best in Mull and takes in the island's second highest hill, Dun da Ghaoithe, the hill of the two winds. The hill welcomes the visitor to Mull as it dominates the approach to Craignure. Perhaps it was named by sailors as it deflects the winds up the Firth of Lorn and Sound of Mull. Certainly its summit and the long ridge leading northwards from it offer an incomparable view of these two stretches of water as well as fine prospects of the central Mull mountains.

From Craignure, take the A849 Fionnphort road and, just past the gates to Torosay Castle, turn off on the right hand side of the road up a narrow cutting. Fork right almost immediately and follow the road until it reaches a locked gate near a farm. There is room to park here.

Cross the sturdy stile, helpfully put there by the landowner, and walk up the road to the first of two telecommunications masts, then on up to the second transmitter tower. The road is very steep but you will want to stop frequently to admire the views across to Duart Castle and beyond to Oban and Lorn. Looking north Ben Nevis, the Mamores and the peaks of Glencoe can also be seen clearly, when the weather is right. By this time you are two thirds of the way up as you strike off due west for the summit of Dun da Ghaoithe, skirting the curved cliff of crags at the head of Coire nan Each. As always, the appearance of a trig pillar is a welcome sight but this pillar and the cairn behind are not yet the summit which lies a quarter of a mile to the NW and 30 feet higher.

Dun da Ghaoithe is at 766m (2513 ft) the second highest of the Mull hills, topping the more spectacular Ben Talaidh by 5 metres and Ben Buie by 49 metres, and is the higher of Mull's two Corbetts. A Corbett is a summit between 2500 and 3000 feet with drop of at least 500 feet all round. Like the Munros, these summits are "collected" by enthusiasts until the total of 221 have all been climbed.

From the summit follow the ridge in a north westerly line, traversing over a series of little tops, rocky mounds and around lochans - Beinn Thunicaraidh, Beinn Mheadhon, to the last top, Beinn a Chreagach Mhor, the first top to dip below 2000 feet. The views change here - the Sound of Mull, which has been a constant companion on the right hand, now swings away directly ahead of you to Tobermory and there are new and spectacular views through the gap made by Loch na Keal to Staffa, Little Colonsay and the Treshnish Islands, northwards to Loch Frisa, up the Sound of Mull to Calve Island off Tobermory and beyond to Ardnamurchan, with the possibility of a glimpse of Rum and Skye on a clear day. Across the Sound lies Morvern and the village of Lochaline, where a mine produces very fine sand for industrial use, and the old and new Ardtornish castles. You may see a small freighter negotiating the narrow entrance to join the ceaseless traffic plying the Sound of Mull: CalMac ferries heading for the Outer Isles, ore carriers taking rock from the Glensanda quarries to engineering projects around the world, smaller cargo boats, fishing boats and yachts of various sizes.

The ridge at this end is by no means as clear as it appears on the map and you should set off downhill from the summit of Beinn a Chreagach Mhor, on a NNW course taking a line on the Green Isles until reaching a rocky knoll immediately above Pennygown Cemetery. The line from here is towards the estuary of the Forsa river which will bring you down to the road near the cemetery after what has been a splendid high level walk. The ruined 13th century chapel is worth visiting (see Mull: *Monuments & History*) before setting off back to your starting place.

Other descents may be made. The first opportunity is to go down the north side of the Allt an Dubh Coire going down the ridge until a deer fence is reached. The gate is across the river just below some fine waterfalls. Re-cross the river and continue down keeping above and to the west of the green fields of Scallastle farm to reach the main road at another gate.

There are several ways to tackle this hill using the buses or a combination of car and bus. A bus service connects with the ferry from Craignure every two hours in summer (see timetable) and buses leave Craignure for Iona on the same basis. It is therefore possible to drop off the ridge at many points and catch one of these buses to return to your starting point. It is also possible from Craignure to reach Torosay Castle by narrow gauge railway or a woodland walk.

13

6. Glen Clachaig

6 miles, 4 hours

For stalking information telephone 01680 300358 or 300380 (Season August-October 20)

This route is one of the ancient drove roads used to move cattle from one part of Mull to another. Beef cattle (usually called 'black' whatever their colour) were the mainstay of the Highland economy up till the 19th century. From as early as the 16th century it is known that cattle were shipped from Coll and Tiree and landed at Croig and Kintra, from there they were driven through the glens of Mull, grazing as they went. In Glen Bellart there was one of the largest fairs in the West Highlands where, three times a year, cattle dealers congregated from all over the country. In the mid-eighteenth century, Mull exported about 2000 cattle a year. Most of these went out through Grass Point and were shipped by way of the island of Kerrera to the mainland. The shortest sea crossings were chosen as well as the best grazing on the way, in order to get the cattle to the trysts (markets) at Crieff and Falkirk in the best condition possible.

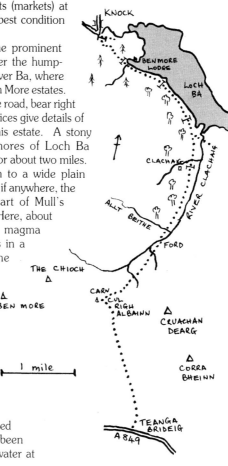

Start at Knock on the prominent bend in the road just after the hump-backed bridge over the River Ba, where the track leads into the Ben More estates. Immediately on leaving the road, bear right through a gate, where notices give details of the stalking season on this estate. A stony track leads along the shores of Loch Ba through old birch woods for about two miles. The valley opens out on to a wide plain surrounded by hills. Here, if anywhere, the explorer feels at the heart of Mull's ancient volcanic drama. Here, about 60 million years ago, a magma reservoir pushed upwards in a huge dome but when the pressure was released through a ring-shaped crack, the centre subsided much like a failed soufflé.

About half-way up the loch, the drove road forks to the right and the route through Glen Clachaig is signposted. The track continues till it crosses a burn below a ruined cottage - the bridge has been washed away, but if the water at

14

the ford is too deep, then there is the remains of an old bridge beside a rowan tree about thirty yards downstream. The next burn, the Allt Beithe, should be crossed close to where it flows into the River Clachaig. Just downstream are two small round stone enclosures. These are sheep buchts or twinning pens where orphaned lambs are bonded to a foster mother. Upstream the ford across the Clachaig river is marked by a small cairn on a level patch of grass, and in wet weather can be knee-deep. Some of the drovers of old were mounted on small ponies, but crossing rivers was always a problem.

By now the Chioch has come into view, dominating the head of the valley, and on the other side of the col is Cruachan Dearg mirroring the Chioch in its conical shape. Walking in the valley bottom is heavy going through the luxuriant moor grass which provides rough grazing for cattle right up to the head of the valley, though the large hairy Highland cattle of today are at least twice the size of the wiry black cattle which were driven over this pass in the old days.

From the ford, the path goes steadily uphill to the top of the pass, with, here and there, the old stone edging of the drove road visible through the grass. In the 18th century, landlords had to provide statute labour for the building and maintenance of roads. The tenants from Lagganulva to Killiechronan worked on this road.

At the summit of the pass (1089 feet) stands the Carn Cul Righ Albainn (Cairn with its Back to Scotland). This cairn is supposed to mark the boundary between the Picts and the Scots. The path from here to the Glen road is well made and descends by a steady gradient, at first through the hanging valley of the Allt Teanga Brideig and then by a sharp descent to the road, with views of the Coladoir River meandering to its estuary at Loch Scridain.

Head of Loch Ba

7. Burg and the Fossil Tree

10 miles, 7 hours
An all-day excursion

MacCulloch's Tree, the fossilised cast of a tree growing over 50 million years ago, was discovered by the geologist John MacCulloch in 1819 at the end of the Ardmeanach peninsula.

From the B8035 take the turning to Tiroran, passing behind Tiroran House. This section of the route is well waymarked by the National Trust until you are delivered safely into the Trust's car park, 2¾ miles along the road (cars may not be taken any further). Despite all this, it is still a walk into untamed scenery - long and at times hard going, but full of interesting geological features and wild land and seascapes. Goats and red deer can be seen and buzzards and eagles hunt along the cliffs. Pass through the gate by the car park and follow the track on past Tavool house, then on another mile to Burg Farm (Chrissie's Cottage).

Just past the farm is Dun Bhuirg, an early fortified structure and one of many duns around the coast of Mull. Within its walls is a memorial to Daisy Cheape drowned on August 15, 1896. The Cheape family owned Tiroran and Carsaig estates and the accident occurred when Daisy, then twelve, her brothers and boatmen set out on a very wild day to sail round to Carsaig. the dinghy taking the party out to embark capsized and all were saved except Daisy. Pause to read her memorial and to look back up Loch Scridain to the saddle-backed summit of Ben Buie.

From here, the path crosses a grassy area, once cultivated, before it begins to climb up and follow the side of the hill. It is a fairly narrow track and requires care in places. Along this stretch some of the unusual formations of basalt columns can be seen. On the island of Staffa these hexagonal columns are mostly vertical but here they lie horizontal, or in a fan shape, in one place like the spokes of a wheel and in another laid down like bottles in a wine cellar. Looking down on these from the path above is more rewarding than the closer view you can get by scrambling down to the shore.

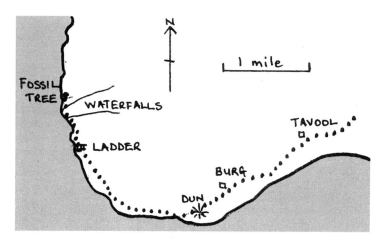

The path now continues at the same level until it ends in a short downward slope (care should be taken) to the head of a steel ladder running down 20 feet of cliff and giving access to the final section of bouldery beach. After that it is a scramble along the shore - agates can sometimes be found here. There are two waterfalls falling down from the high cliffs in parallel symmetry. These, which can be seen from as far away as Iona, are markers for the tree which lies just beyond. The outline of the trunk is moulded in the lava face to the left of a cave mouth and the shape and size of this trunk, 40 feet high and 5 feet across, is that of a massive tree. This tree was large enough to exert a cooling effect on the lava by which it was engulfed with the result that the surrounding columns of basalt have been bent towards it. At the base, about four feet from the ground, there can be seen the dark charcoal remains of the timber from when it was overwhelmed by hot lava, and at one time much more of this black deposit was visible. Eroded by fossil hunters over the years, only the hollow shape now exists. Please do not be tempted to damage this unique fossil any further.

From the tree the usual route back is to retrace your steps along the shore, up the ladder and along the path to Burg and Tiroran.

It should be noted that going beyond the tree is a major undertaking - the headland being only negotiable at low water or by a difficult and potentially dangerous route further up. The north side of the peninsula is some of the most broken and difficult country in Mull.

One of the twin waterfalls

8. Ben Buie

717 m, 2352 ft

Restricted period mid-August to mid-October

Ben Buie is another of the hills on Mull that gives the climber the total satisfaction of starting from sea level and climbing every one of the 2352 feet to the summit. It dominates the loch and village which carry the same name - buidhe (boo-ee) meaning yellow. Its glacis of grass and scree rising to a summit dome of crag is unmistakable as you come down the winding road to Loch Buie. What is not evident from the road is that there are, in fact, two summits and that the area between them and to the NE of the second summit is a terrain of lumpy ground crossed by little rock bands. In mist this broken country is confusing and the fact that crags and cliffs await the unwary on SW, SE and E sides makes the top of Ben Buie a bad place to get lost: there is a local magnetic anomaly and the compass should not be relied upon.

Leave the Lochbuie road at the telephone box and follow the fairly well worn route up the left side of the burn, crossing some smaller burns on the way. Height is quickly gained on the continuously steep slope and each pause for breath will give you time to admire the widening views of the waters of Loch Buie. At the head of the loch you will see Laggan Sands, Moy Castle and the wide spread of level ground behind Lochbuie House. As you get higher, Loch Uisg comes into view to the south-east and there is a wide panorama over towards Oban and Lorn.

From about 1700 feet, rough scree demands careful footwork to avoid starting an avalanche of stones. The last 100 feet look formidable from below and gazing upwards the walker may be excused for wondering whether there is a way up through the crags which girdle the summit, but there is a shallow rake running from left to right which takes you to within a few feet of the southern and higher top. The summit cairn is a fairly substantial one and affords shelter while you admire the wide views of the other hills of Mull. Across Beinn nan Gobhar to the west you can see Gorrie's Leap, at the top of the high cliffs above the Carsaig Arches. To the north lies Ben More while to the north-east are Cruachan Dearg, Corra Bheinn and Ben Talaidh, all inviting climbs some other day.

Descent by the steep route of the ascent is rather remorseless and a more varied way down may be found by walking across to the second summit a quarter of a mile away. From the second summit continue north, to avoid the precipitous east face and pick your way down into Coire nan Each. Before going down, it should be possible to see the line of descent almost clear to the valley floor at the southern end of the loch. Here you are joining the old path through from Glen More to Lochbuie and the return to the road is described on page 20.

Ben Buie

A Beginner's Hill Flora

For anyone just starting to take an interest in plant life, the hill country of Mull is a good place to begin. The acid soils and the high rainfall produce a distinctive flora with few surprises and, for the beginner, reassuringly few species. The budding botanist, taking to the Mull hills should be able to tick off the following 50 species without delaying the rest of the party and pronounce them typical of the western hills of Scotland.

Ten for starters
Ivy
Foxglove
Honeysuckle
Rowan
Harebell
Thyme
Bracken
Cross-leaved Heath
Bell Heather
Ling

Plants of the hill slopes
Heath Bedstraw
Bilberry
Bugle
Cowberry
Eyebright
Hard Fern
Parsley Fern
Herb Robert
St John's Wort

Heath Spotted Orchid
Early Purple Orchid
Sea Plantain
Devil's Bit Scabious
Selfheal
Heath Speedwell
Tormentil
Bird's Foot Trefoil
Bitter Vetch

Plants of the tops
Alpine Ladies Mantle
Cat's Foot
Moss Campion
Sea Pearlwort
Rhacomitrium (Moss)
Roseroot
Selaginella Selaginoides
Starry Saxifrage
English Stonecrop
Thrift

Water Plants
Bog Bean
Potomogeton Sp
Water Lobelia

Plants of the boggy ground
Bog Asphodel
Butterwort
Cottongrass
Sun Dew
Grass of Parnassus
Lousewort
Bog Myrtle

9. Circuit of Ben Buie

12 miles, 7 hours

Restricted period end August - end October

This long circuit round the base of Ben Buie, the highest hill south of the Glen More road, gives a fine appreciation of the desolate country around Glen More, that great glacier-gouged slice through Mull which separates north and central Mull from the Ross and the extreme south.

Leave the A849 at Ishriff, 10 miles from Craignure, above the chain of three lochs. Walk down to the isolated dwelling house, then continue down to Loch Sguabain. Follow the west shore of the string of lochs as far as the open ground between Loch an Ellen and Loch Airdeglas then cross the burn to the east side where a good path goes all the way to Loch Buie. The long eastern flank of Ben Buie rises steadily on the walker's right hand all the way.

In the shallow col the path crosses some boggy ground and in two places a series of stepping stones has been laid at some time, as useful now as when they were put in position. Just before the path starts its final descent to Loch Buie it crosses the Abhainn a'Chaiginn Mhoir and the walker should be alert not to miss the crossing place. The path passes close to a distinctive pyramidal mound. Ford the river about 50 yards beyond. The path now descends sharply between large black ice-smoothed rocks. From here you can see down to the flat lands round Lochbuie, and out to sea lies the island of Colonsay, with Islay and Jura beyond. There is a ruggedness about this last mile of descent - the Gleann a'Chaiginn Mhoir, or valley of the rough terrain - and at the point where the path joins the road, Ben Buie presents its most spectacular aspect, girdled with crags and dominating the few houses at its feet. The path meets the road through a metal gate 20 yards east of a fine old stone bridge.

With the use of two cars it is possible to terminate the walk here. There is much of interest to see at Lochbuie. See page 22.

To continue the walk, turn right where the path joins the road and walk over the bridge and past the houses of Lochbuie. The road reaches the sea at a curious triangular monument erected by Lochbuie and his Highlanders to commemorate the coronation of King Edward VII and Queen Alexandra. Turn right again here and continue until, just after a burn is bridged, there is a gate and a sign indicating the public footpath to Carsaig. However, turn right yet again and go up the hill to some farm buildings and out onto the hillside beyond. Climb steadily through the woodland for about half a mile until below the craggy end of Beinn nan Gobhar. The path now forks, one path leading gently down and along the wall (see page 23, the Horse Track), the right-hand fork leading up the hill. Keeping ever to the right, now tackle the rise up to the Bealach an t-Sidhein (pass of the fairies) pausing, as you will feel the need to do quite regularly, to look back at the view of Loch Buie and beyond. Once Loch Buie has disappeared you will have the satisfaction of knowing that the hard work of ascent has been done. For the next mile the walker works gently round the contour with the crags of Ben Buie to his right and the dramatic valley of Glenbyre to his left.

When the head of the valley is about half a mile off, the crags come to an end and there is a minute and reedy lochan to the right of the path. You should leave the path at this point and make for the summit of Cruach nan

Con (1626 feet). Ben Buie, lost to view since turning up Glenbyre, comes back into sight, now showing its western aspect over the waters of Loch Fuaran. To the left of it is the symmetrical top of Ben Talaidh and the weary walker may be interested to know that his car lies directly below it. But if at this point he thinks the rest is a formality, he is sadly mistaken. The descent from Cruach nan Con over Torr a Ghoai into the valley of the Abhainn Loch Fuaran (itself a problem in spate) and the walk down to the road are the roughest two miles in the whole round. Even the sheep do not reckon much to this as walking country and you are left to plough your own pathless and trackless way through the endless hummocky moraines until you finally reach the valley floor and are faced with the choice of fording the Coladoir River or following it up to the watershed between it and the River Lussa. There is no bridge now at Craig. Only the fine panorama of the hills north of the Glen road relieves this last section and the tarmac was never so welcome as on the last stretch back to the car. An excellent round despite the sting in the tail.

10. Short excursions around Lochbuie

1. Laggan Sands and Mausoleum

Shortly after passing Loch Uisg on the road to Lochbuie there is a lodge and white gates. Turn left through the gates and then left again, where the road forks. Follow the twists and turns of the road down to the sea, turning left yet again at the junction where the sea is reached. The wide sweep of Laggan Sands are a quarter of a mile beyond, backed by the open grassy space where the car may be parked.

The Mausoleum for the MacLaines of Lochbuie is an interesting objective for a short stroll from the beach. The chapel is mediaeval in origin but had fallen into disuse by 1701, the date of the first burial. It was considerably restored in 1864 and again in 1972. It may be reached by the track that runs along the top of the beach.

2. Moy Castle

Although Moy Castle is within easy walking distance of Laggan Sands, the more usual approach is from the end of Loch Buie village. From the Post Office, follow the track east along the shore to a small car-park. Continue down the track, over the bridge, through the field gate and along the marked path. The castle, although apparently in a good state of preservation, is unsafe and is kept locked for that reason. This MacLaine stronghold dates from at least the early 15th century and continued to be lived in until 1752 when the new mansion nearby was built. This is a private house and not open to the public.

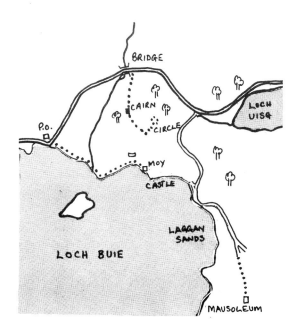

STONE CIRCLE
LOCHBUIE

3. Stone Circle

This is the only stone circle on Mull. The circle consists of eight stones with the place of a ninth marked by a boulder and an isolated stone a few feet away. There are also two other stones in the vicinity and a kerb cairn in a group of trees.

To reach these monuments, keep on for the houses of Lochbuie past the turning for Laggan Sands and leave your car at the stone bridge over the Abhainn a'Chaiginn Mhoir. Go through the wicket gate and walk across the field following the direction of the white stones and crossing a small wooden bridge in the field (there is a standing stone some distance to the left of this). The circle lies behind the rhododendrons and once this has been visited, it is worth deviating towards the line of trees on your left to visit a kerb cairn which is located in the clump or grove in this line. This whole area was obviously of great significance in prehistoric times.

4. The Horse Track

The shore road to Glenbyre was built at the beginning of the century, carved out from the rugged and broken coast. The older route in was by the 'Horse track.' This pleasant short walk starts near Lochbuie Post Office. Walk westwards along the shore road to a bridge over the burn where the walk to Carsaig is signposted. Go through the gate on your right immediately after this and go up the hill to the farm passing above the outbuildings and out onto the hillside beyond. This is also the start of the old right of way over the hill to Rossal. After half a mile the path goes through a gap in a wall and across a burn with the craggy end of Beinn nan Gobhar rearing up ahead. Fork left here, following the wall downhill and into the oak woods. The path runs down through a wooded valley and along through the trees some 100 feet above the shore. This is a delightful walk, a secluded high-level promenade among the trees which, after about a mile brings you out at Glenbyre. Once you leave the trees, the way down is indistinct, but the roof of Glenbyre farmhouse can be seen below and the path comes down a gully just a little short of it, immediately opposite the third telegraph post on the Lochbuie side of the house. If you do not wish to go so far, you can cut down to the shore road by a steep path that takes off just before the end of the trees above an area striped with old cultivation ridges. A small cairn is a marker for the descent. A brief stroll back along the coast road completes a very attractive walk.

THE WALKS

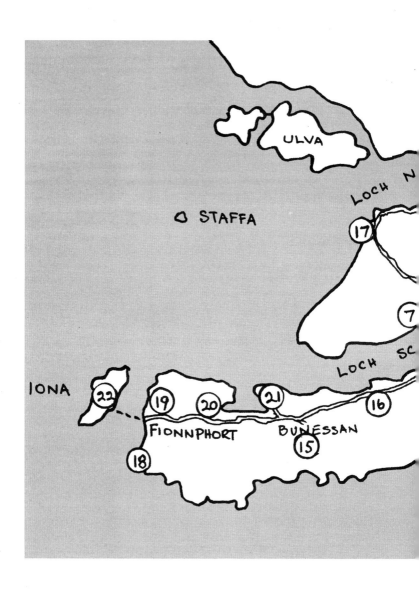

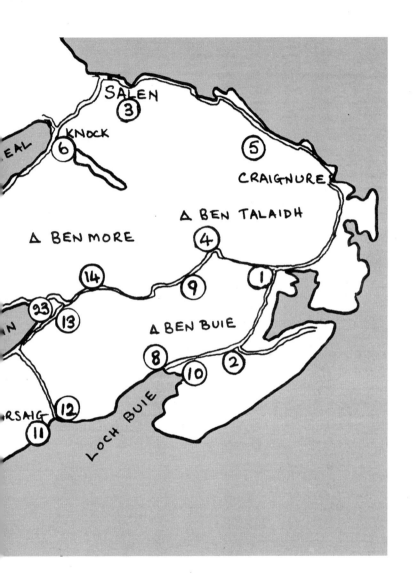

SALEN
③

KNOCK
EAL
⑥

⑤
CRAIGNURE

△ BEN TALAIDH

△ BEN MORE
④

⑭
⑨

①

㉓
⑬

△ BEN BUIE

⑧
⑩
②

ȠSAIG
⑫

⑪

LOCH BUIE

11. Carsaig Arches

8 miles, 6 hours

This is one of the most spectacular walks in south Mull. The Carsaig Arches are not merely one of the wonders of Mull - the four mile walk out to them passes below cliffs that are breathtaking in their height and scale and tenanted by wild goats, ravens and eagles. They are, however, four very long and rough miles and, in certain conditions of sudden thaw, some danger may be expected from rockfalls.

The Carsaig cliffs from Carsaig pier

Starting from just above the pier at Carsaig, take the track through the trees and round the shore of the bay. The track degenerates and two burns must be crossed but once the western side of the bay is reached, the path is reasonable and planks have been laid over the worst of the muddy places.

About an hour's walking brings you to the Nun's Pass, the only place in a three-mile stretch of coastline where the great rampart of cliff is breached and a steep grassy slope gives access to the moorland above. A curious Sphinx-like rock stands on the shore below the pass and a little on the Carsaig side of this, tucked in behind a low bank is the Nun's Cave where the nuns are reputed to have taken refuge after being driven from Iona. Crosses of various designs, some of which may go back to the 6th-9th centuries are carved on the walls. These must be picked out from amongst much ugly modern graffiti. There are also several dates, the earliest being 1633, a carving of a sailing ship, and mason's marks which date from the time when this cave was used by stonemasons working the sandstone cut from the tidal stretch just in front of the cave. This easily worked buff or greenish stone was used in parts of Iona Abbey and other church buildings. These quarries were worked from the early middle ages and thereafter intermittently throughout the centuries, the last re-opening being in 1875 when stone was used in the restoration work at Iona Abbey.

Another hour brings the walker to the arches, the scenery getting increasingly grand with waves breaking over the rocks and distant views to Jura, Islay and Colonsay. Above is a jagged skyline with crumbling cliffs soaring up to nearly a thousand feet. Beyond Malcolm's Point the path comes to an abrupt and dramatic end above a rock inlet where the sea rolls in towards the first and more massive of the two arches.

Once this arch has been sufficiently admired and photographed from this point, the walker should retrace his steps to a small stream where a goat track leads up the gully and up over the the arch - a good and level path but affording no protection whatsoever against the sheer drop to the sea. One step off the path would put the walker in a totally irretrievable position, but this is the only way to get down to the beach and stand beneath the great arch. These arches were originally sea caves which have been eroded right through the rock to form a tunnel and the great arch is 140 feet from one end to the other. The second of the two arches is taller and more slender and sports a stack at the top like a chimney.

The return can be made by the same route or, outside the stalking season (mid-August to mid-October, see note 3 on Deer, Page 4) by continuing a little further steadily climbing towards Gorrie's Leap (Binnein Ghorrie) the next break in the rampart of cliff. This also is not a route for the faint-hearted and it is best to climb as high as possible on the east of this gully before entering it to avoid too much scrambling in this very loose and unstable ground. Gorrie was a clansman of MacLaine of Lochbuie who, when savagely punished by his chief for a trivial offence, took terrible revenge by seizing Lochbuie's baby son and, with the baby in his arms, leapt to destruction off the top of the cliff.

The walk along the top of the cliff is pleasant and easy. At the lowest point of the cliffs where a stream goes over the cliff with a wall beyond it, Gamhnach Mhor comes into line with the east point of Rubha na Faoilinn. This is the top of the Nun's Pass. Descend the pass and return along the shore to Carsaig Pier.

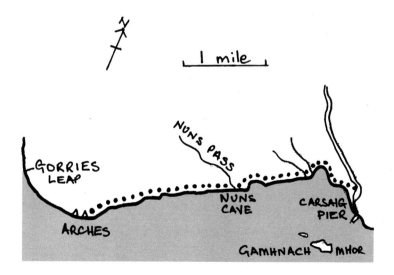

12. Carsaig to Lochbuie

6 miles, 3 hours

This is one of the best known walks in south Mull, taking you along a varied and interesting shoreline. The distance by car from Carsaig to Lochbuie is twenty-five miles, along the shore route a mere six, and in times gone by it was a well maintained route. Now, however, the sections of constructed path may be measured in feet rather than yards.

Start from Carsaig Pier at the notice "Public Footpath to Lochbuie." At first the path is enclosed as it passes through woodland and in places is muddy, but planks and stones help you to avoid the worst spots and the sea is soon reached. The section from here to the isolated stack called An Dunan is the most spectacular on the walk as you pick your way between the hollow cliffs and the sea. On windy days the rock face throws back the echo of the sea. Shallow caves, carved by the sea in the time of higher sea levels, run in under these cliffs, some with walls built across the entrance to be used as sheep fanks.

Beyond An Dunan the path switches between the rocky shore and the wooded skirts of the cliff. There is a sharp contrast between the wild coast with its tidal pools, and the sheltered dells where the stones are covered with thick and prolific moss. At the edge of the sea are oyster-catchers and cormorants while the woods are home to tits and wrens.

The going gets harder in the centre section of this walk, with some scrambling among the boulders, especially at high tide, to avoid the sea spray thrown up canyons and clefts in the rocks. At An Cui'Leim a rib of rock runs out preventing further progress by normal means and there is a piece of rope slung down a ten foot drop to help walkers negotiate this place when the tide is in.

After this, the walking becomes easier and more open, with the cliffs further back from the edge of the sea. The walker is now coming in from an exposed coast to a sheltered and peaceful bay where the vegetation is more lush and the shoreline less dramatic. Just before Glenbyre there are two fields with a bridge over the Glenbyre Burn in the top corner of the first of them. From the farm a good track takes you the last mile and a half to Lochbuie.

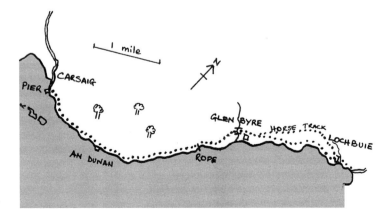

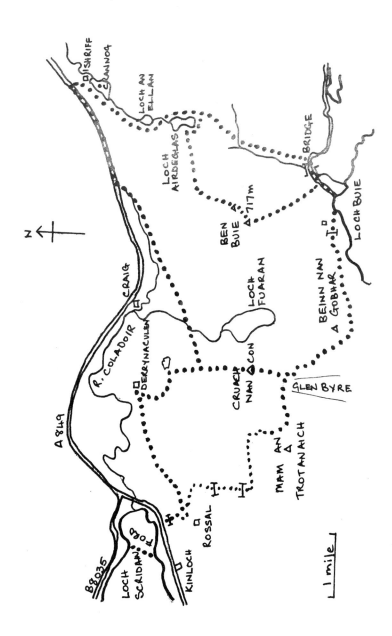

BISHRIFF
CANNOQ
LOCH AN EILLAN
LOCH AIRDEGLAS
BRIDGE
717m
△
BEN BUIE
LOCH BUIE
BEINN NAN A GOBHAR
LOCH FUARAN
CRAIG
R. COLADOIR
DERRYNACULEN
CRUACH NAN △ CON
GLEN BYRE
MAM AN △ TROTANAICH
A849
ROSSAL
KINLOCH
B8035
LOCH SCRIDAIN
LOCH BEG
N ←
1 mile

13. Rossal Circuit
Rossal to Loch Buie

7 miles, 5 hours

5 miles, 3 hours

Park the car near the head of Loch Scridain - a convenient place on the A849, Craignure to Iona road, may be found just east of the bridge over the Allt a Mhaim, about halfway between the Kinloch Hotel and the junction with the B8035, where there is a section of old road. Bus passengers should ask to be put off at the Rossal road end.

Walk up the farm lane and go through the gate. Just short of the farm, turn left on to the forestry track until, on reaching a fank, take the track up the hill to the right. Some way up this, a gate gives entrance to a forestry plantation. The old route to Glen Byre is signposted about 10 minutes walk from the gate but a better route is to continue on the track until it ends. From there a well trodden footpath takes you on to a gate and uphill through the trees. Keep on this track as it slants eastwards along the contour until you reach a junction marked by a small cairn. Bear right and carry on until beyond the plantation and out onto the open hill - from here the Mam Trotanaich is within easy reach. On top of the pass, the walker is rewarded with the fine views towards Loch Buie and over the Firth of Lorn. Traverse eastwards along the contour, taking a line on the summit of Ben Buie if fine, and in mist lining up the two cairns at the top of the pass as your direction, to make for the dramatic gash which marks the head of Glen Byre.

From here, if you do not wish to retrace your steps, you have several options. You may, if a two-car arrangement has been made, drop down to Loch Buie by following, in reverse, the route down the east side of Glen Byre described in paragraph five of the Ben Buie Circuit keeping well up under the crags of Beinn nan Gobhar. Alternatively, a circuit may be completed by ascending Cruach nan Con, as described in paragraph six of the Ben Buie Circuit and then dropping down the western side of Torr a Ghoai to the attractive small Lochan na Cruaiche. From here it is most important to choose the correct line of descent as two forestry deer fences stretch right around the foot of the hill from Rossal to the Abhainn Loch Fuaran.

There are no stiles, gates or other means of crossing these fences but there is a gap between them directly above Derrynaculen: a corridor of hill which can be reached by setting off directly due west from Lochan na Cruaiche. A prominent boulder on the skyline is a marker for the route down, but it must be emphasised that the walker should keep well up - heading for the mouth of Loch Scridain. Do not be tempted to skirt the base of the Cruach Doire nan Cuilean, as this will lead you over the lip of the Leathad Mor - in Gaelic, the great slope, though the great wall might be a better description for this face of precipitous slab and vertical vegetation. Over it flows a very fine waterfall and the four streams which feed it run in deep gullies. Keep up and, in mist, count them carefully before beginning the descent. The steep but grassy slope of the Leathad an Fola sweeps down to the forestry road between Derrynaculen and Rossal. Turn left on this road, pass through the gate and so back to Rossal.

14. Ben More from south   *966m, 3169 ft*

Ascent over Chioch and Chioch ridge

The first part of this ascent follows, in reverse, the route described on pages 14 and 15, climbing steadily up from Teanga Brideig in Glen More on the old drove road. From the historic cairn at the top of the pass, follow the broad ridge to the foot of the Chioch. Once the first few feet of scree are surmounted the footing is by no means as uncomfortable as it appears from below, though walkers should be aware of the dangers of dislodging loose boulders and keep close together or follow separate lines up the slope.

The summit is, as it appeared, the apex of a pyramid. The change of view now embraces the country to the north and east of Ben More - the undulating ridge of Ben Fhada with its craggy little summit, and the wide corrie between Ben Fhada and Ben More of which the Chioch ridge forms the back wall. This ridge has been compared to a miniature Aonach Eagach but this, though it pays tribute to the fine rocky character of the ridge, is something of an exaggeration of its difficulties. In fact, the walker makes his way along a sort of rampart with a protective wall of rock rising on one side with the occasional window looking north. However, the southward sweep into the Corrie Odhar is impressive enough for those with poor tolerance to exposure and in windy or icy conditions the ridge should be treated with respect.

The ridge ends in a final pull up a steep rocky slope onto the summit of Ben More. It is not always clear which route the path takes at this point but there is a small, shallow gully on the south side of the hill which offers reasonable footing a good part of the way up. A final burst brings the walker tumbling right over the east side of the summit shelter cairn and lands him precipitant and puffing amongst the sandwich-eaters who have already attained the top from the easy side.

Summit of Chioch and Chioch Ridge

Descent to the south

From the summit of Ben More, more than one route of descent is possible, though the route over the Chioch ridge is probably best only as an ascent. The most popular route to the summit starts at sea level at Dhiseig but this descent is only possible with two cars. For the walker who started at Teanga Brideig and came up over the Chioch, a descent to the south is the best variation and more or less completes a circuit.

From the summit cairn, set off due south along an open plateau with the ground falling away dramatically to the left. After the cairn, the direction turns to the south-west and the descent becomes steeper. The walker reaches Maol nan Damh after picking his way across a stretch of ground scattered with little lochans. Turning south again the descent is a steady but steep route over rough ground broken by large slabs of rock to reach the B8035 near Loch Beg. from here turn left and follow the road to just short of the Kinloch junction,turning left again to follow the old road most of the way back to Teanga Brideig.

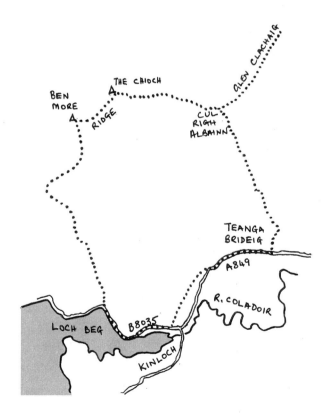

15. Scoor

9 miles

An all-day excursion

An exploration of the south coast of the Ross of Mull, returning over moorland tops which, for all their modest height, give wonderful views back to the hills and out to the isles.

Turn off the Craignure-Fionnphort road just short of Bunessan, where Assapol House and Scoor are signposted. Park at the visitors' car park just above Kilvickeon cemetery and continue on foot on the track that leads to Scoor House. Bear left to pass in front of the house and go through the gate. The track carries on for a while, climbing uphill to enter a field with a fank in it. Ignore the gate below the fank and cross the field to the top gate, continuing until the ridge is breasted, then turn left along the ridge making for the forest ride, conspicuous across the valley. In a short while, the track to Shiaba will be spotted below you and in a few yards along this you will see the gable end of a building said to have been the schoolmaster's house. Over 350 people lived here at the end of the eighteenth century and the remains of their houses and the boundary walls that marked their crofts can be seen.

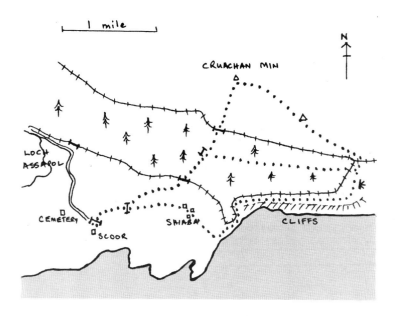

Then came the clearances and from the beaches below the emigrant ships took the people away and the sheep moved in. Now it is the turn of the forestry - a deer fence enclosing young trees now bars further progress in a straight line and the walker must descend to the shore to skirt it, unless he is prepared to cut across forestry ridges from the end of the new wall to get to the top of the cliffs. As compensation for this forced descent, the walker may be interested to know that the isolated ruin here is the shop which served Shiaba, sited close to the shore for the landing of goods in bulk. The deer fence now runs back up the hill and the walker, following along the outside of it quickly, if somewhat sharply, regains the high ground - a place to have your binoculars ready for deer, eagles and wild goats - everything, in fact, that gives south Mull its unique atmosphere. It is a most exciting place to be, but there is a fairly narrow strip of ground between the fence and the clifftop and attention should be paid to where you are putting your feet as well as eagle spotting.

Eventually the deer fence turns inland and you can either follow it to a point where it has been taken down where a faint track connects with the forest road down the middle of the plantation or continue onto the high ground and look across to the cliffs running out to Malcolm's Point and soaring almost 1000 feet above the Carsaig Arches just visible at their foot. Halfway along where the highest point of the visible horizon juts out like a platform is Gorrie's Leap. If you want to make your way to the arches from here, make the descent to the shore by the gully west of Eas Criarachain waterfall as described in Walk 16.

Now it is time to turn inland, returning to the deer fence and following it till you reach a gap which will take you out onto the higher moorland where, with height gained, all the hills of Mull come into view to the north-west. The trig pillar is not quite the highest point but the ridge from there to Cruachan Min is easy striding on well-cropped heather. Once arrived, you can start counting islands - Islay, Jura, Scarba, Lunga and the Islands of the Sea (Garvellochs), Luing and Mull, Colonsay, Staffa, Coll, Iona and Tiree. All present and correct and on a clear day you can also tick off Barra Head and, by straining your eyes and imagination, the Cuillins.

The homeward route is through a wide firebreak where the old forestry marches with the new (there is a gate to get in at the top and another to get out at the bottom). At the bottom you come out into a shallow valley where the MacPhees from Colonsay once attempted a raid on Shiaba. They were to sail from Colonsay under cover of darkness but, too eager for the fat cattle of Shiaba, set off with last rays of the setting sun catching their boats. The Mull men were waiting in ambush in this valley and fell on the MacPhees, routing them and taking prisoners. These were sent home to Colonsay but not before each had had his thumbs cut off to make sure that it would be no easy task to row back again. A gloomy tale if you are late off the hill, but the Shiaba track is just across the other side of the shallow valley and the last mile back to Scoor house is familiar from the route out.

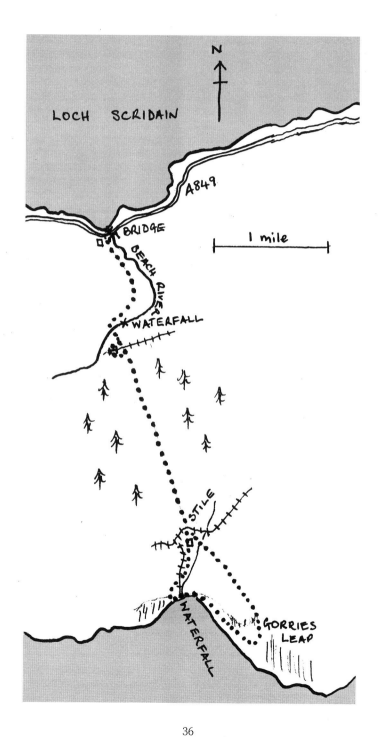

LOCH SCRIDAIN

N

A849

BRIDGE

1 mile

DEACH RIVER

WATERFALL

STILE

WATERFALL

GORRIES LEAP

16. Across the Ross

7 miles, An all-day walk

Stalking Season: See Code for Mull on page 4

This walk passes easily through open country and woods and ends with an awesomely wild second section. Those who decide to the complete circuit must be prepared for some scrambling. As with the walk to the Carsaig Arches, there is danger from rock falls in conditions of heavy rain or sudden thaw.

Start at the bend in the A849 where it crosses the Beach river: there is ample parking between the road and the sea. Cross the river by the old bridge and follow the Land-Rover track that passes below the bungalow and out onto the moor through a gate. The walking is less monotonous than one might be led to expect from the map and there is a fine waterfall in the eponymous Allt an Easa Mhoir. The track goes through a shallow ford at the top of the waterfall. A hundred yards on, pass through a side gate into the forestry plantation. Within the plantation the walking is reasonably open as the trees do not crowd the road and the planting is mixed with spruce, larch and pine. There is a tempting view ahead to the spectacular rock bastion of Ben Gorrie - a rugged hilltop surmounted by a turret of rock. The view of this clifftop gets more dramatic as the walker goes on.

At the end of the trees, a good stile takes the walker over the deer fence and onto an older but still firm track, and soon the sea comes into view. As the path splits, bear to the right towards a group of ruins. These are named on the map Airigh Mhic Cribhain, but all appear to have been more substantial buildings than one would expect of an airigh or sheiling. A sheiling was a dwelling used only in the summer when the cattle were taken to more remote pastures to graze, away from the growing crops. Here, too, the women would make butter and cheese. The buildings were usually small huts roofed with heather and the remains found today are often scanty. In this group there is also evidence of a stackyard and a corn-drying kiln. Those with an interest in deserted villages may well feel happy to have reached journey's end. Those whose taste runs more to geological time rather than historical should prepare to descend to the shore down through the layers of the tertiary volcanic ages.

From this group of buildings walk to an old fence which runs down towards the burn. Then continue, with the fence on the right and the burn on the left. Where the fence crosses the burn, cross the fence (but not the burn) and carry on to the top of the cliffs. Suddenly, you will come to the top of a waterfall, the Eas Criarachan, but it may announce itself earlier by clouds of spray if a strong wind is blowing up the cliff.

After admiring the views of the cliffs and sea and distant islands from this airy vantage point, the walker can either retreat and retrace his route to the start, or extend the walk by descending to sea level. Work eastwards along the cliff to find a steep gully leading clean down to the shore (though there is quite a lot of loose scree in the middle to negotiate, so keep together if walking in a group).

From the bottom it is possible to pick a way back along the shore to the waterfall and round into the deep bay called Traigh Cadh an Easa, which offers a stretch which is easier on the ankles. The cliffs soar above the walker and on windy days the sound of the sea echoing off the steep face can be quite deafening.

Beyond, the going is slightly easier if the walker navigates along the aerial trackways of the deer and the wild goats who are the proper residents of this domain (it is claimed that the goats have been there since the days of the Spanish Armada). These game trails run across the slope almost like visible contour lines, but by working gently upwards from one to another the walker will slowly gain height. All the time, though, the cliff top is gaining height until at Gorrie's Leap its crenellated lip is over 900 feet above the sea. You begin to feel you have entered a lost world and if you do not see a pterodactyl come over the cliffs you will very probably see an eagle.

Gorrie's Leap (for story see page 28) is the last possible way back to the world above for the next three miles and the game trails lead faithfully up it - the centre hump between the two washouts is probably the easiest route. Once at the top, the Airigh Mhic Chriabhan is not difficult to pick out. As you walk down the slope you may be interested to know that there is a seam of inferior coal nearby which has been casually worked in recent times. From here it is down the slope and back to the track to amble home, enjoying the open views across Loch Scridain to Ben More and the other hills of central Mull

With two cars, it is possible to link this walk with the Carsaig Arches or Scoor.

17. MacKinnon's Cave   *2 miles*

A short but energetic walk with a little scrambling in places. As the cave is only accessible from about half-tide, it is essential to check the tide-tables for the day to avoid a wasted journey..........or being cut off. You should also take a torch (no daylight penetrates the innermost recesses of the cave) and keep your dog on a lead till through the gate at the top of the cliffs.

Leave the B8035 just beyond the Gribun rocks where the road begins to climb into Glen Seilisdeir, and go down the farm road. Park the car just short of the cattle grid at Balmeanach and walk up to the farm, bearing left to skirt the farm buildings and avoid the fields below the farm. Pass through a gate beside the outbuildings and follow the fence on your right to the top of the cliffs. Dogs should be kept on a lead across this field. A small gate above the sea at the far end of the field gives access to the shore. A winding track leads downwards and a short quarter-mile along the coast of increasing drama brings you to the cave. Everything here is on a grand scale including the flotsam - there are some huge logs, part of a cargo which floated in the sea for some time and were the subject of a sécurité warning to shipping before they came ashore. Just before the cave there is a waterfall and then some large rocks washed by the tide at the mouth of the cave which have to be scrambled over or around.

At just over 500 feet, MacKinnon's cave is reckoned to be the deepest in the islands. Boswell and Johnson visited it on their tour in 1773. As befitted eighteenth century inquirers, they measured it painstakingly - and with surprising accuracy, considering that their measuring instrument was a walking stick and they only had one candle. They were not, however, impressed by the legend associated with the cave. The story goes that a group of people headed by a piper went into the cave never to return. Only the piper's dog returned some hours later, crazed with fear and - the most terrible detail of all - without a hair on its body. Go quietly  and perhaps you will hear the ghostly wail of the pipes.

The return from the cave is best made by the same route, taking time to admire the cliff scenery and the view out to Staffa.

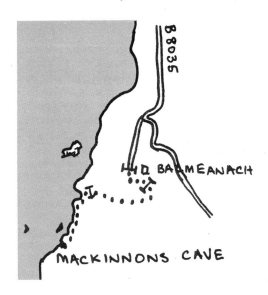

18. Erraid

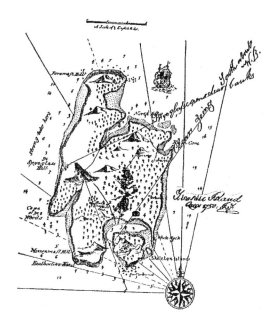

A visit to a tidal island with literary associations.

For those who have read Kidnapped, Erraid will always be the island where the shipwrecked David Balfour to his chagrin spent four wet and miserable days living off shellfish because he did not realise that the island was tidal. But Stevenson used the island in other stories as well and, on a sparkling day in spring or summer one might believe his early acquaintance with the emerald seas, the pattern of reefs and the warm red rocks of the Ross of Mull fired his imagination for the South Seas and the story of Treasure Island, the chart of which, "struck out by J Hawkins" bears more than a little resemblance to Erraid.

At low tide you can walk down from Knockvologan Farm and cross the sandbank between the low granite cliffs dryshod. The channel is about a quarter of a mile in length and should be continued to its northern end and round the coast to the buildings that formed the shore base for the construction of Dhu Heartach lighthouse. The houses and outbuildings were built for the lighthouse keepers and their families and the present day occupants use the gardens and storage to be similarly self-sufficient. Skirting round these it is an easy climb past the disused signal station to the highest point (no trig pillar now) and stand imagining how it must have felt to be marooned on this island with neither food nor shelter as described in RLS's story.

He was one of the great Stevenson family of lighthouse engineers and as a student he spent time here during the building of the lighthouse. This light, which may be seen 15 miles out to the SW is 126 feet high and marks a treacherous rock less than 50 feet above sea level in the middle of the passage up the Firth of Lorn. Closer to you are the notorious Torran rocks where David Balfour was wrecked and between the outermost of the islands to the SW you may see yachts lying in Tinker's Hole, the last secure anchorage for boats heading southwards round the Ross. Across the water lie the marble quarries of Iona and, to the NW the Abbey, always a conspicuous landmark in the southern part of Mull.

From the top of the hill return by striding across the heathery uplands and around the granite torrs to reach the sandbank crossing before the tide comes in (tide tables can be obtained from chandlers and shops).

David Balfour continued his adventures by walking across Mull, presumably through Glen More, though Stevenson takes some writer's liberties with distances and has him meet a selection of colourful characters on the way before he finally reaches the inn at Craignure (then called Torosay).

19. Fionnphort Quarries *2 miles, 1 hour*

The Fionnphort or Tormore quarries are only a short walk from the Iona ferry landing place. This is one of six quarries that were operating in the Ross last century.

A quarter of a mile along the main road from Fionnphort village is a track leading north past Bruach Mhor. The track goes up the hill behind the buildings and almost immediately you come upon the old quarry workings. The quarry was closed about 1910 and until 1987 there were huge blocks of cut granite, some seven feet by four feet, stacked ready for shipment at the point when commercial working stopped. Recently the quarry has been re-opened, the blocks removed and some limited working takes place. Further exploration brings you to the main quarry area, where a long tramway led down to the pier. The stone was once exported to many parts of Britain, and even the USA, before competition and transport costs grew too high. It may be seen in London, Liverpool and Glasgow: the Holburn Viaduct, the Liverpool Docks and Jamaica Bridge were constructed using this rich pink granite, which was also used extensively in buildings throughout Mull for facings and lintels.

Just off the pier is a safe anchorage known as the Bull Hole, sheltered by Eilean nam Ban (Island of the Women), to which Columba is said to have banished women from Iona, suspecting they might cause trouble!

Return to the start of the walk by the same route.

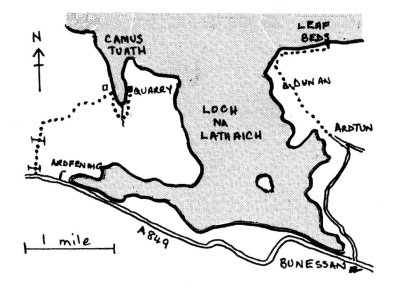

20. Camus Tuath

3 miles, 2 hours

Another short outing in the Ross of Mull.

Leave the road half a mile west of Ardfenaig where a gate just past a footbridge opens onto a track. Follow this track north across the open moorland. After half a mile the track bends to the right through rocky outcrops and soon a fine wall, built 'Galloway' style, borders the track all the way down to the bay called Camus Tuath. An adventure camp for young people makes use of the old buildings near the shore, originally built to house workers at the quarries across the bay.

The actual quarry workings can be reached by making your way round the inlet crossing the saltings at the head. In the quarry drill holes and other evidence of working can be clearly seen. The remains of the tramway lead down the hillside from the quarry to the pier from which the granite was shipped. This is still in reasonably good order being built of this hard stone. The granite here is a pale flesh colour, not as pink as that from the quarries at Fionnphort and has a coarse-grained texture. Blocks were used to build the Skerryvore (1844) and Ardnamurchan (1849) lighthouses which were designed by Alan Stevenson, uncle of the writer Robert Louis. The Skerryvore reef, pounded by the full force of the Atlantic, lies 10 miles south-west of Tiree, right in the path of vessels making for the Clyde and Mersey and the lighthouse which marks this hazard can be seen from one of the walks on Iona (see page 45).

Return to the start by crossing the head of the inlet again and then go round the hill and make for the gap in the wall to rejoin the track.

21. Ardtun
2 miles, 1½ hours

This is a short geological excursion from Bunessan with easy walking. The leaf beds of Ardtun were first described by the then Duke of Argyll in a paper in The *Quarterly Journal* of the Geological Society of London on January 8, 1851. They are composed of the leaves of (mainly) deciduous trees, falling autumn after autumn into the waters of a prehistoric lake and there becoming fossilised by a process so gentle that even today the leaf beds resemble nothing so much as narrow bands of leaf mould set between gravels and sand.

From Bunessan take the road signposted to Ardtun and follow this till you come to a fork. Bear left along the road by the shore and park on the right-hand side, just before the last two houses are reached where the road goes over a culvert. From here, the most attractive course is to walk to the little flat-topped outcrop of Dunan Mor with its conspicuous cairn. Carry straight on, descending to the shore. The most interesting way follows the coast, though there is an easier and less dramatic route along the top of the little cliffs.

On the lower route there are interesting coastal features, notably stands of columnar basalt. In the distance you may see Staffa where columnar basalt is to be seen at its most impressive and regular. Sheep tracks take you along under the low basalt cliffs, passing round the precipitous head of a chasm with the sea surging into it and bringing you to a deep, narrow inlet - likewise precipitous at the head. Here you are forced up to regain the top of the cliffs. Now cut across the headland looking north-eastwards towards the soaring mass of Ardmeanach. In a very short while you will reach the top of another gully easy of access at its head. This gully is completely dry, well above the sea and strewn with fallen rocks.

In the sides of this valley are the fossilised leaf beds which were first seen for what they were by the Duke of Argyll. The leaf beds are visible as recessed bands where years of scraping by fossil hunters have worn the layers away. Samples represent a temperate flora with leaves of hazel, plane and oak trees and are indicative of the climate here in the Eocene era (about 54 million years ago).

Return by the same route - the moor is wet, boggy and generally less attractive than the shore.

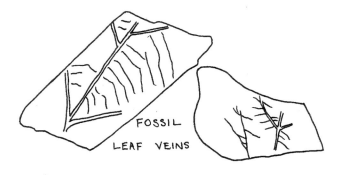

FOSSIL LEAF VEINS

22. Iona

The sacred Isle of Iona is known throughout the world and thousands of people visit it every year, making a pilgrimage to its ancient abbey and precincts. This is all well described in other guides and not within the scope of this book. The island is a small piece of the Outer Isles dropped off at the end of the long arm which is the Ross of Mull. The distinctive pink granites of the Ross cease at Fionnphort and Lewisian gneiss, the rock of the Western Isles, takes over to form, in Iona, an island of humps and hollows: "little rocky hills, with narrow verdant hollows between...numerous enough for every recluse to take his solitary walk, undisturbed by society," says Thomas Pennant, who visited Iona in 1774 - a walker's quotation to stand beside that of a more famous visitor: "That man is little to be envied, whose patriotism would not gain force upon the plain of Marathon, or whose piety would not grow warmer among the ruins of Iona" (Samuel Johnson).

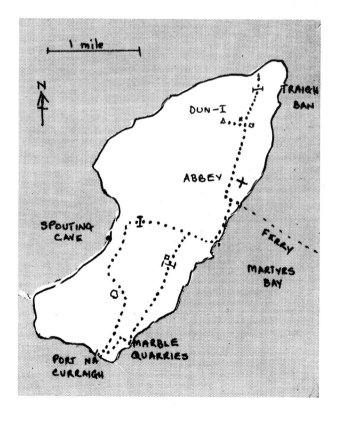

Walk 1

Leaving the ferry, turn left and follow the tarmac road past Martyrs Bay and Traigh Mor. Continue on the road as it turns up the hill and comes eventually to a gate. Through the gate you come on to a stretch of machair - short, springy turf growing on a base of windblown shell sand. Machair is a special habitat found on the Atlantic coasts of the islands of Scotland and, being rich in lime, affords sheep and cattle good grazing. Here you will see one or two holes of the little Iona golf course.

Bear left and make towards the pebbly shore to look across to the Spouting Cave, a natural curiosity from which, with a good westerly swell running, a burst of white water and a plume of spray rises high up the cliff. When the cave is in good form this plume can be clearly seen from the summit of Dun-I, two miles away.

From the shore, follow the track that leads due south over the hill, keeping the lochan on your right and then on down to Port na Curaich, known as St Columba's Bay. It was here that St Columba landed in his coracle in 563 AD. A long mound of earth is said to mark the size of his boat and shingle from the shore has been heaped to form a multitude of cairns - no one knows the age or origin of these, though another tradition has it that these were the penitential cairns of monks, set to raise heaps equal to their sins.

Before leaving the bay, a hunt along the beach could produce little green pebbles but, if disappointed here, a visit to the marble quarries might yield a small piece of Iona marble with, perhaps, a small vein of the green serpentine for which the marble was once so famous.

To find the quarries, climb up over towards the eastern shore of the island, pausing to look back out to sea to the west, where the Skerryvore Lighthouse (built 1844) can be seen on the horizon. Continue above the shore till you come to a hollow where there are two ruined cottages and below, in the deep gully, you will see the skeletal remains of a producer-gas engine manufactured by Fielding & Platt, of Gloucester, and a cutting-frame by G. Anderson, of Arbroath. The structures remaining are a small dam cut into the rock and a gunpowder store. At the water's edge a steep-sided rock acted as a landing-stage in calm weather for boats taking away the stone. Rusty stanchions are still firmly embedded in the rock. The quarries were worked at various times from early days, the last period of activity lasting from 1907 until shortly after the outbreak of the first world war. The walker who wishes to see a really impressive slab of Iona marble should now return to the centre of the island (taking a bearing on Dun-I, the highest point on the island will bring you out at a farm called Ruanaich). There, in the heart of the island, the communion table of the Abbey Church is entirely constructed of marble from these quarries.

Port na Curaich

Walk 2

Another walk on Iona is to the top of Dun-I itself. Continue on the past the Abbey till the farm called Auchabhaich is reached (there is a pebble-dash building with a corrugated iron roof on the right-hand side of the road). Turn left up the track at the side of the building opposite and then up the rocky hillside. From the top of Dun-I the island is spread out around you and the hills of Mull and other more distant islands, such as Jura and its three Paps, can be seen.

Returning to the road by the same path, you can explore a little farther by turning left and walking along till you reach the beautiful white sands of Traigh Bhan, another of Iona's lovely beaches.

Marble Quarries

23. Kinloch Ford

It seems fitting to end this book with a short walk that finishes at a pub. The Kinloch Ford was used to cut off the two miles round the head of Loch Scridain. Rapid and exceptionally thirsty walkers can even beat the car round to the pub if dropped at the north side of the loch directly opposite the Kinloch Hotel. Walk alongside the spit of land until you come to a post - the route lies between this post and the post on the south side in front of the hotel. In the days before the motor car, this was a well-used route for carts, animals and people on foot. When the Coladoir is in spate, the middle of the ford will be knee-depth and it goes without saying that this should only be attempted at low tide!

Further Reading

Other publications from Brown and Whittaker:
Walking in North Mull Companion volume to this.
A Walk Round Tobermory, The history of Scotland's smallest burgh, illustrated by six short walks in and around Tobermory.
Mull, Monuments and History: An excursion guide to standing stones and archaeological sites.
Mull, Natural History: An excursion guide introducing all the main natural habitats of the island.

Novels and Films
Annabel Carothers, *Kilcaraig*. Family saga of three generations of Mull landowners. A good read.
Elisabeth Luard, *Emerald*.
Robert Louis Stevenson, *Kidnapped*. (Walk no. 18)
Archie Roy, *Sable Night*. Supernatural thriller set on Mull.
"I know where I'm going" Cult movie (1945) starring Wendy Hillier (Walks no. 10 & 12).

Natural History Reference Books.

J.E. Richey, *The Tertiary Volcanic Districts*.

Richard Fitter, Alastair Fitter and Marjorie Blamey, *The Wild Flowers of Britain and Northern Europe.*

A.C. Jermy and J.C. Crabbe, *The Island of Mull, Flora* (British Museum, 1978). Detailed and specialised.

Hermann Heinzel, Richard Fitter, John Parsloe, *The Birds of Britain and Europe.*

P. Hayman, *Birdwatchers Pocket Guide*. Well-produced and, in slim format, truly a pocket guide.

Mike Madders and Philip Snow, *Birds of Mull*.

Hamlyn Guide, *Seashores and Shallow Seas of Britain and Europe*.

Whittet Guides: *Otters, Deer, Eagles, Puffins, Seals, Whales*.

Larousse Pocket Guides.

General Mull

HMSO: *Argyll 3* (Mull, Tiree etc), and *Argyll 4* (Iona): The Royal Commission on the Ancient and Historical Monuments. Detailed and specialised.

N. Hesketh, *The Story of Mull and Iona*. A historical interpretation through the eyes of an artist.

P.A. Macnab, *Mull & Iona*.

Alastair de Watteville, *The Isle of Mull*.

Christine Wiener, *Mull, A Traveller's Guide*.

Jim Crumley, *The Heart of Mull*.

Nicholas Maclean-Bristol, *Warriors and Priests*, the History of the clan Maclean, 1300-1570.

P.A. Macnab, *Highways and Byways in Mull*.

Tall Tales from An Island. traditional, historical, supernatural or just personal anecdotes.

D.M. MacQuarrie, *The Placenames of Mull*. A useful book for Highland placenames, generally.

Relevant to specific walks (walk nos. in brackets)

Samuel Johnson & James Boswell, *Journey to the Western Islands of Scotland and Journal of a Tour to the Hebrides* (17, 22).

Scott MacAdam, *The Great Mull Air Mystery*. An account of the mysterious disappearance of Peter Gibbs on Christmas Eve 1975 by a local plane enthusiast. (4).

Joan Faithfull, *The Ross of Mull Granite Quarries* (19, 20)

David Viner, *The Iona Marble Quarry* (22).

Robert Louis Stevenson, *The New Lighthouse on the Dhu Heartach Rock, Argyllshire* (18).

Other walking guides

SMC: *The Munros*
The Corbetts
The Islands of Scotland including Skye.

First published 1987

Printed by
Printworks Oban